# Phoenix Rising: The Journey from Ashes to Empowerment

Master the art of healing trauma, rebuild your trust and strength, and manifest a life you deserve.

By: Lisa Bennett, Ed.S

## Preface

"In the depth of winter, I finally learned that within me there lay an invincible summer." — Albert Camus

This poignant reflection by Albert Camus captures the heart of transformation—the journey from despair to empowerment. My intention is to guide you not just through coping but toward deep, foundational healing that reconnects you to your inner strength.

In these pages, we'll explore the difficult terrains of past traumas and cycles of abuse that may have clouded your life's experiences. This book is born of both personal trials and professional insight, rooted in the belief that everyone deserves to lead a life filled with hope, love, and trust.

While growing up under challenging circumstances, I encountered adversity early: addiction, toxic relationships, and personal upheaval were recurring themes in my life. These experiences profoundly shaped my understanding of trauma and recovery. Through them, and my subsequent academic work in psychology and counseling, I gained the tools—and the empathy—to help others navigate similar struggles.

Throughout these chapters, you'll meet individuals who, like you, once felt overwhelmed and disconnected. Their stories demonstrate how rebuilding trust in oneself can lead to thriving, healthy relationships and a fulfilling life.

Take Sarah, for instance. After enduring years of emotional abuse, she struggled to trust her own judgment. Through the strategies outlined in this book, Sarah reconnected with her inner strength, ultimately creating healthy, loving relationships. Or consider James, whose unaddressed childhood trauma manifested as severe anxiety. By confronting his pain with understanding, he began a journey toward self-confidence and peace.

These stories inspired this book and underscored the need for a comprehensive guide to healing. The strategies you'll find here are designed to help you understand your past traumas, navigate grief, and rebuild your mental, emotional, and physical well-being.

I'm grateful for the mentors and colleagues who have enriched my journey with wisdom and support. Their insights have shaped this work, and I hope this book becomes a supportive guide for you in your own journey.

As you turn these pages, I acknowledge the courage it takes to face your pain and reclaim your power. Remember, within you lies an invincible summer waiting to emerge from the shadows of winter. Let's begin this transformative journey together and manifest the life you truly deserve.

## Chapter 1: Unraveling the Chains of the Past

"The wound is the place where the Light enters you." — Rumi

## Can We Ever Outrun Our Shadows?

Julia walked through the bustling farmers' market, her steps light but her thoughts heavy. Though the air was crisp and fragrant with ripe fruit, her mind lingered on the shadows of her past. Each stall offered vibrant displays of tomatoes, sunflowers, and artisanal breads, but Julia struggled to stay present.

She paused at a display of plump red tomatoes, their smooth skin reminding her of rough hands that once promised safety but delivered pain. The contrast was striking, almost too much to bear. Setting the tomato down gently, as though it were made of glass, Julia took a deep breath.

Nearby, a child tugged his mother's skirt, his wide eyes alight with wonder at an array of sunflowers. Julia lingered, watching their faces turn toward the sun. How, she wondered, could she reclaim that light within herself?

When an old song floated through the market, its cheerful melody transported Julia back to a time before her life was marred by trauma. But as nostalgia gave way to sorrow, she realized: the past could not be erased, only rewritten.

## Breaking Free from the Echoes of Yesterday

Trauma leaves more than scars—it reshapes how we see ourselves and the world around us. Like Julia's story, it can entangle us in cycles of fear and self-doubt, making it difficult to distinguish the past from the present.

But here's the truth: though trauma may shape your starting point, it doesn't have to define your destination. By understanding how trauma distorts your personal narrative, you take the first step toward reclaiming your life.

## Understanding Trauma's Grip

Trauma disrupts life's natural flow, trapping you in a cycle of re-living pain. It clouds perception, turning everyday interactions into reminders of past hurts. Recognizing this distortion is crucial—it allows you to step back and see that what feels overwhelming is often a shadow of something long gone.

For example:

•Do you find yourself overreacting to small   setbacks?

•Are you constantly on edge, even in safe environments?

These signs indicate that trauma is still influencing your inner world. By identifying these patterns, you can begin to untangle the chains holding you back.

**Reclaiming Your Story**

Healing starts with rewriting the internal scripts trauma has created. This process involves acknowledging your pain, but also reframing it as a story of resilience. Each small step—whether it's asking for help, setting boundaries, or practicing self-compassion—moves you closer to freedom.

In this chapter, we'll explore strategies to:

1.Identify how trauma has shaped your perspective.

2.Develop tools for emotional regulation.

3.Create a personal narrative rooted in strength, not victimhood.

Through reflection, practice, and courage, you can break free from the shadows of your past and step into the light of your true self.

## Chapter 2: Embracing the Waves of Recovery

"It is not the strongest of the species that survive, nor the most intelligent, but the one most responsive to change." — Charles Darwin

**When Healing Feels Like Breaking**

Mara walked through the park, her footsteps soft on the carpet of autumn leaves. A cool breeze tugged at her scarf, an unspoken reminder that the seasons were changing once more. Around her, children's laughter rang out—a stark contrast to the turmoil within her.

She had been told countless times that healing isn't linear but more like the rhythm of waves: retreating and returning with varying intensity. Knowing this, however, didn't ease the frustration she felt when old memories resurfaced. Today was such a day—a day when the tide of her past seemed stronger than her present footing.

Sitting on a worn wooden bench, Mara's eyes wandered to an elderly couple walking arm in arm. Their synchronized movements reflected decades of shared endurance, and she wondered about the storms they had weathered together.

Her thoughts were interrupted by the joyful shriek of a child racing past her bench, his mother following with laughter. The sight stirred something in Mara: a blend of longing and tentative hope. Perhaps healing, she realized, wasn't about avoiding the waves but learning to stand resiliently within them.

## Understanding the Unpredictable Rhythm of Healing

Healing from trauma is often depicted as a steady climb from darkness into light. In reality, the process is filled with peaks, valleys, and unexpected turns. This journey can be frustrating, but embracing its non-linear nature is crucial for building resilience and self-compassion.

Think of healing as a zigzagging upward path. Each peak represents progress—a breakthrough moment or a positive day. Each valley, though difficult, is not failure but a necessary part of growth. The goal isn't to avoid setbacks but to understand them as opportunities for deeper healing.

By shifting your mindset to accept this rhythm, you free yourself from the pressure of perfection and instead focus on persistence. Healing isn't about how fast you move forward; it's about continuing to move forward, no matter the pace.

## Navigating Setbacks with Strength

Setbacks are an inevitable part of the recovery journey, but they don't define you. Instead, they offer a chance to learn more about yourself and your needs.

Here are strategies to help you navigate setbacks:

1.**Pause and Reflect**: Take a moment to step back and assess the situation. What triggered this setback? What emotions are surfacing? Reflection can turn setbacks into valuable learning experiences.

2.**Reconnect with Your Strengths**: Remind yourself of past victories, no matter how small. This reinforces your capacity for resilience and helps you regain perspective.

3.**Lean on Your Support Network**: Reach out to trusted friends, family, or a therapist. Sharing your experience can reduce feelings of isolation and offer new insights.

4.**Revisit Your Tools**: Whether it's mindfulness, journaling, or grounding techniques, lean on the coping strategies that have worked for you in the past.

## Chapter 3: From Brokenness to Wholeness

"You are not a drop in the ocean. You are the entire ocean in a drop." — Rumi

## Can One Truly Integrate Trauma Without Losing Themselves?

Anna sat at her kitchen table, the steam from her tea curling like tendrils of thought. Outside, the city hummed a quiet tune—a backdrop to her internal reverie. She held the mug close, feeling its warmth seep into her palms, mirroring the slow thawing of memories she had kept frozen in the recesses of her mind.

Her eyes shifted to the window, where children played under the watchful eyes of autumn leaves, whispering secrets before they fluttered to their demise on the concrete below. Anna's thoughts drifted back to her childhood—vivid yet fragmented scenes that EMDR therapy had helped resurface. The therapy sessions were like delicate surgery for her soul, each memory carefully dissected and reintegrated, reducing its sting but not erasing its essence.

She recalled her therapist's words from earlier that week, "Integration is not about forgetting, Anna. It's about reshaping your story so you can hold your past and still move forward." These words floated around her now like a melody that both soothed and unsettled.

The kettle hissed in the background, pulling Anna back from her reverie. She rose to pour another cup when a sudden clatter at the door startled her. Her heart raced—a reflex not yet tamed by therapy. She opened it to find a neighbor's child, ball in hand, apologizing for the loud thud against her door. A simple interaction to most, but a test of resilience for Anna; she managed a smile and reassured the child with kindness.

Returning to her seat with fresh tea in hand, she noticed how each sip tasted less bitter than before therapy began. It seemed each session dissolved another layer of hardened distress that flavored her life experiences.

As dusk fell and shadows grew longer across her kitchen floor, Anna pondered if this integration meant acceptance or surrender. Was she molding herself around trauma or truly moving beyond it?

## The Power of Integration

Trauma by nature fragments us, shattering the coherence of our life story. Its broken pieces often echo through our everyday existence, distorting how we see ourselves and the world. Healing requires more than simply "moving on" or burying the past; it involves gathering these pieces and carefully placing them within a broader, more compassionate narrative of who we are.

This process of integration isn't about erasure. It's about reframing the trauma so that it no longer controls us, yet remains a part of our story—one that no longer defines our identity. Rather than forgetting, it's about transforming the painful memories into lessons of resilience.

Therapies like Cognitive Behavioral Therapy (CBT) and Eye Movement Desensitization and Reprocessing (EMDR) serve as powerful tools in this process. They don't wipe the memories away—they allow us to revisit them safely and with new perspectives, reducing their emotional intensity and helping us to live in the present.

Imagine your life as a tapestry torn by trauma. Integration is the act of mending it—not to hide the scars, but to weave the story of endurance, courage, and eventual strength into the fabric.

### Reducing Trauma's Emotional Grip

To regain control over your future, you must first loosen trauma's emotional grip. This involves transforming your relationship with the past, moving from reactivity to reflection. It's not about avoiding emotions, but rather about learning to manage them constructively.

Here's how to loosen trauma's hold on your emotions:

1.**Recognize Emotional Patterns**: Pay close attention to how certain memories or triggers affect your emotions. Are there recurring themes, responses, or reactions? Awareness is the first step toward change.

2.**Practice Mindfulness**: Use grounding techniques to help you stay present when painful emotions arise. Focus on your breath, or engage your senses by noticing the colors, sounds, and textures around you. The goal is to stay anchored in the present rather than being swept away by past hurts.

3.**Reframe Your Narrative**: Instead of seeing your trauma as something that broke you, see it as a challenge you survived. This shift in perspective can transform your pain into power. By reframing the trauma, you reclaim ownership of your story.

4.**Seek Professional Guidance**: Therapeutic techniques like EMDR or CBT can be instrumental in processing unresolved emotions. A therapist can guide you through the integration process, helping you build a stronger connection to your present self.

Healing doesn't erase what happened—it helps you reclaim your power over how it shapes you.

**Empowering Choices and Reactions**

Trauma often robs us of our sense of agency, leaving us feeling powerless. Reclaiming this agency is essential for moving from brokenness to wholeness. The power of choice—of reclaiming control over how you respond to life's challenges—lays the foundation for healing.

To regain control over your reactions and choices, try these strategies:

1.**Set Boundaries**: Boundaries are essential for protecting your emotional energy. Setting healthy limits with others and with yourself ensures that you can focus on healing and that your space is respected.

2.**Build Emotional Resilience**: Strengthen your ability to weather emotional storms by developing tools like journaling, mindfulness, or gratitude practices. These strategies help you process difficult emotions and maintain stability, even in the face of challenges.

3.**Celebrate Small Wins**: Progress may feel slow at times, but every step forward, no matter how small, is a victory. Acknowledge your efforts and celebrate each milestone—getting out of bed, going for a walk, or simply breathing through a tough moment.

Each small, intentional action empowers you to reclaim your life. Over time, these actions will help you reshape your relationship with your trauma, turning it from a source of pain into a source of strength.

## From Survival to Growth

Healing isn't just about surviving—it's about thriving. It's about using your trauma as a stepping stone for personal growth, moving from a place of pain to one of strength and purpose. This chapter is about transforming pain into purpose and using your experience to fuel your future.

Ask yourself these questions:

• What strengths have I developed because of what I've endured?

• How can I use these strengths to shape a future that is meaningful to me?

By focusing on growth, you shift from the question of "Why did this happen to me?" to "What can I create from this?" This shift in perspective is where the real healing begins, as you take back control of your narrative and move from surviving to thriving.

## Chapter 4: Small Steps to Rebuilding Trust

"Trust yourself. Think for yourself. Act for yourself. Speak for yourself. Be yourself. Imitation is suicide." — Marva Collins

## A Promise in the Morning Light

Elena stood at the kitchen window, her gaze fixed on the gentle sway of oak branches in the early morning breeze. The steam from her coffee cup fogged up a small circle on the glass, blurring the green hues into a watery canvas. Today marked exactly one year since the accident that had shattered more than just bones; it fractured trust and certainty within her.

As she sipped her coffee, its warmth contrasted sharply with the chill seeping through the windowpane. Her mind drifted to those first weeks of recovery, filled with pain and helplessness but also an unexpected clarity about who she could rely on. The promises made in hospital rooms were like delicate threads, some holding strong while others frayed silently.

In this quiet morning moment, Elena contemplated a new commitment she had set for herself: to walk to the park alone by week's end. Such a simple act, yet laden with layers of fear and doubt she wished to peel away gently. It was less about reaching the park and more about trusting her body—and fate—once again.

Her cat Milo brushed against her leg, pulling her back from spiraling thoughts. She bent down to stroke his soft fur, each movement grounding her further in the present. Milo purred contentedly under her touch, unaware of his role as an anchor in Elena's tumultuous sea of recovery.

Outside, neighbors began their day; doors shut softly and cars murmured to life. Each sound was a reminder of life moving forward, indifferent to individual struggles yet strangely comforting in its predictability.

Could small steps like today's lead Elena back to a place of trust within herself?

## Is Rebuilding Trust Truly Possible After Trauma?

Rebuilding trust after experiencing trauma is like nurturing a delicate seedling in a storm-swept garden. It requires patience, gentle care, and most importantly, small yet consistent steps that foster growth and strength. When trauma disrupts your life, it can shatter the very foundations of trust you once held, not only with others but also within yourself. This chapter will guide you in regaining that lost trust through manageable commitments to yourself and gradual outreach toward others.

Trust is the cornerstone of all relationships—it's also the lens through which we view ourselves and our capacity to engage with the world. Post-trauma, this lens is often clouded with doubt and fear. Rebuilding trust starts with acknowledging the natural hesitations but also recognizing that small actions, when repeated consistently, can begin to clear away the fog.

### Understanding the Gradual Process of Rebuilding Trust

Rebuilding trust is inherently gradual. It's like restoring a broken bridge—each small act of reliability adds a brick to a new structure, brick by brick. Initially, the process may seem daunting or even impossible, but remember, trust is built over time through consistent actions, not grand gestures.

The first step in rebuilding trust is accepting that it's a process, not an event. Trust takes time to develop, and it requires consistency, transparency, and respect. To begin, start with yourself. Commit to small promises and follow through. These small commitments are the foundation upon which larger trust—both with others and within yourself—will be built.

## Implement Small, Manageable Commitments to Stabilize Self-Reliance

The rebuilding of trust with oneself begins with small, achievable steps. These manageable commitments reinforce the belief in your ability to follow through, which is essential for trust. For instance, committing to write in a journal for five minutes each day, or setting aside time each morning for self-care, may seem simple but can have a profound effect on how you view yourself and your ability to heal.

Imagine your life as a garden. Each small commitment you make is like planting a seed. Just as a seed needs regular watering to grow, each commitment needs attention to bear fruit. This process doesn't just nurture your trust in yourself—it strengthens your belief in your ability to take care of yourself.

By keeping promises to yourself—no matter how small—you prove that you can rely on your own actions. This consistency forms the cornerstone of your self-trust and begins to heal the wounds of self-doubt caused by past trauma.

## Understand the Gradual Process of Rebuilding Trust with Others

Rebuilding trust with others follows a similar process, albeit with an added layer of vulnerability. Initially, it can feel overwhelming to trust someone again, particularly if past relationships have been marked by betrayal or hurt. However, trust with others is not restored all at once. Just as you rebuild trust with yourself through small actions, rebuilding trust with others requires gradual, consistent steps.

Start by engaging in small acts of trust. It might be sharing a thought or feeling with a close friend or asking for help with a simple task. These small exchanges are the first steps in reinforcing that trust. Trust is built when others demonstrate reliability, respect, and understanding—qualities that are earned, not given.

### Setting Boundaries to Foster Trust

Setting boundaries is a vital part of rebuilding trust—both with yourself and others. Boundaries are not walls that isolate you; they are protective measures that ensure your emotional and physical well-being. Healthy boundaries define what is acceptable and what is not, and they help prevent the erosion of trust that can occur when boundaries are ignored.

For example, you might set a boundary by limiting time with individuals who do not respect your emotional needs or by clearly stating your need for space when overwhelmed. Establishing and maintaining these boundaries allows you to regain a sense of control and respect in your relationships, which is crucial for rebuilding trust.

**Celebrate Small Wins and Progress**

Rebuilding trust is a journey that involves both setbacks and victories. Recognizing and celebrating small wins is crucial to staying motivated and continuing forward. Every time you keep a commitment to yourself, every time you set and honor a boundary, every time you speak openly with someone, you take a step closer to rebuilding trust. These small victories might feel insignificant in the moment, but over time, they add up to substantial progress.

**The Path to a Life Filled with Empowerment and Trust**

Rebuilding trust—whether with yourself or others—is a gradual process that takes time, patience, and commitment. But with each step, you are rebuilding your foundation, one that is sturdy, resilient, and capable of supporting a life of true empowerment.

Remember, trust is not a destination—it's a journey, one that you navigate with courage, honesty, and perseverance. By taking small steps, setting boundaries, and building reliability through consistent actions, you will gradually reclaim your ability to trust yourself and others again. Each day you invest in this process, you pave the way for a future filled with deeper connections, empowerment, and lasting fulfillment.

## Chapter 5: Aligning Dreams with Reality

"The future belongs to those who believe in the beauty of their dreams." — Eleanor Roosevelt

**Can Healing Align with Hope?**

Eva walked through the park, her steps slow, measured against the crunch of autumn leaves beneath her boots. The crisp air brushed against her face, a reminder of the changing seasons, much like the changes she sought within herself. As a survivor, she often found her inner desires at odds with the harshness of reality. Today was no different.

She sat on a worn wooden bench overlooking a pond where ducks glided effortlessly across the water. Their ease in movement contrasted sharply with the turmoil she felt inside. Eva closed her eyes and breathed in deeply, attempting to ground herself in the moment. Her therapist had suggested using positive affirmations as stepping stones toward reconciling her internal conflicts with external realities.

"Today, I choose to find strength in my scars," she whispered to herself. The words felt heavy, laden with a burden yet to lift entirely, but lighter than yesterday—a small victory in her ongoing battle.

Around her, life continued unabated. Children laughed nearby, their joy unencumbered by past traumas or future anxieties. A couple argued softly on a nearby path, their frustration palpable but contained within the bubble of their mutual existence. Eva watched them momentarily, pondering how they communicated their needs and desires so openly.

She remembered days when voicing even a simple need felt like scaling an immense cliff face without ropes or support. Setting clear goals had been recommended as another tool for recovery—defining what she wanted from life could help bridge the gap between her internal world and external actions. Today's goal was simple: just be present.

As she sat there, allowing herself to just "be," thoughts of future aspirations began to weave themselves into her consciousness—dreams of returning to school, perhaps studying psychology to help others like herself find their paths through trauma.

The sun began its descent behind the trees, casting long shadows across the grass and onto Eva's lap. She stood up slowly, each movement deliberate and filled with intention—her daily practice of aligning action with desire.

As she walked back through the park gates toward home, one question lingered in her mind: How can we build lives that honor both where we have been and where we hope to go?

## From Vision to Reality: The Journey of Transformation

The path from enduring trauma to achieving empowerment is rarely straightforward. It requires not just the healing of past wounds but also a harmonization of one's deepest desires with the often harsh realities of life. This journey, though intensely personal, follows a universal truth: alignment between internal aspirations and external circumstances is essential for true empowerment. For those who have faced trauma, reconnecting with personal desires isn't just beneficial; it's necessary for active participation in life.

### Singularity Moments: The Instant of Transformation

Throughout the healing process, there are pivotal moments when everything clicks into place. These are your singularity moments—the breakthrough shifts where your internal desires and external actions align in a profound, almost instantaneous way. It's the instant when you realize, not just intellectually but in the core of your being, that you can create the life you've dreamed of, despite the scars of your past.

A singularity moment doesn't always come with fanfare. Sometimes, it's a quiet realization in a moment of calm. It might happen when you finally trust yourself enough to make a decision that aligns with your true desires, or when you step forward in faith that your dreams are within reach. These moments are turning points where you move from the abstract idea of healing to the embodied experience of transformation.

For Eva, it was when she sat in the park, allowing herself to simply be, without the constant need to "fix" everything or rush to the next step. It was the moment when she realized that healing didn't mean perfection—it meant integration. Her scars were part of her strength, and they were not obstacles to her future but the foundation of it.

Singularity moments mark the intersections where what you've been working toward comes into alignment with who you are becoming. These moments help propel you forward, marking the transformation from surviving trauma to thriving and manifesting the life you deserve.

**Identifying Desires Post-Trauma**

The first step in aligning dreams with reality is to reconnect with your deepest desires—those parts of you that may have been silenced or lost in the wake of trauma. Trauma can significantly alter how we perceive our wants, often placing a barrier between us and our true aspirations. This can make the process of rediscovery seem daunting, but it is a critical step toward healing.

Imagine your desires as a garden. Under normal circumstances, the garden flourishes, its vibrant colors visible in the sunlight. But when trauma sweeps through, the garden becomes disheveled, the plants buried beneath debris. Recognizing which dreams survived the storm and which need nurturing back to health is essential. This process of introspection, though challenging, helps you sift through the noise of past pain to uncover what truly matters.

Therapeutic methods such as journaling, art therapy, or talking with a trusted friend or counselor can be invaluable in this rediscovery process. These techniques help you to give voice to the parts of yourself that trauma has tried to silence. With each expression, you move closer to a clearer understanding of what you truly desire in life.

### The Power of Affirmations and Goal-Setting

Once you've identified your desires, the next step is to begin setting goals that are aligned with those aspirations. Positive affirmations play a crucial role in this process. They are not just empty words but powerful tools for reshaping your belief system. By repeating affirmations like "I am worthy of the life I dream of," you slowly begin to internalize these messages and release the doubts that hold you back.

Goal-setting, when done mindfully, provides a concrete path to turning your dreams into reality. Start with small, achievable goals—ones that feel within reach. This process of setting and achieving goals fosters a sense of control and accomplishment, helping you move from feeling stuck to empowered.

**SMART goals—Specific, Measurable, Achievable, Relevant, Time-bound**—are a helpful framework for ensuring your goals are realistic and motivating. They break down larger dreams into manageable chunks, making the journey less overwhelming and more focused.

### Crafting a Cohesive Plan

Once your desires are identified and your goals are set, the next step is to stitch these aspirations into the fabric of your daily life. This is not about achieving everything at once, but about creating a sustainable plan that integrates your inner world with your outer actions. It's about aligning your present choices with the future you envision.

Start by breaking down your larger goals into daily or weekly action steps. If your dream is to go back to school, for example, a small, manageable step might be researching programs or setting aside time each week to study. These incremental actions add up over time, helping you build momentum toward your larger vision.

The key is consistency. Aligning your actions with your dreams takes time, but it's the act of showing up daily, even in small ways, that leads to transformation.

### Facing Obstacles with Resilience

As you work toward aligning your dreams with reality, obstacles are inevitable. Old wounds may resurface, or life circumstances may shift. But with each challenge, you have the opportunity to strengthen your resilience.

Embrace setbacks as opportunities for growth rather than as failures. Reflect on the progress you've made so far, even if it feels small. Each time you move through an obstacle, you're proving to yourself that you are capable of creating the life you desire. Healing isn't linear, but with persistence and resilience, every step forward brings you closer to the future you've envisioned.

**Celebrating Progress and Reflecting on the Journey**

Healing and aligning your dreams with reality isn't about a final destination; it's about the journey itself. Along the way, take moments to celebrate progress—big or small. Reflect on the strength it took to reclaim your dreams and the courage to pursue them, even when life feels uncertain.

**Final Thoughts: Living a Life of Alignment**

By identifying your desires, setting goals, and aligning your actions with your dreams, you can move from surviving to thriving. This chapter isn't about denying the struggles you've faced, but about using those experiences to fuel your transformation. You are capable of not just surviving the aftermath of trauma, but of creating a life that reflects your true potential.

Incorporate your dreams into your daily life. Align your choices with the person you want to become. And remember, every step you take is a victory, every moment you live authentically brings you closer to your empowered future.

## Chapter 6: Cultivating Emotional Resilience

"Resilience is not about bouncing back, it's about bouncing forward." — Christine Caine

## The Quiet Strength of Resilience

Zara stood at the edge of the lake, watching the water ripple gently with the evening breeze. The sun, now a golden ball sinking behind the horizon, cast long, soft shadows across the shore. There was a quiet beauty in the scene, but it also reflected the turbulent emotions she had been navigating for months. Trauma had left her feeling scattered—like pieces of herself strewn along the shore, waiting to be gathered, reassembled, and restored.

Her therapist had spoken often of resilience, the inner strength that enables us to face adversity without crumbling. But Zara wasn't sure if she believed it. Resilience had always seemed like something distant, reserved for others who weren't so weighed down by the past.

Yet, standing here, she realized that maybe resilience wasn't about never feeling the weight of trauma, but about learning how to carry it.

Her thoughts were interrupted as the breeze lifted, stirring the water more vigorously. She could feel the wind in her face, pushing her hair back and making her eyes squint against the light. In that moment, she realized something crucial: resilience wasn't about fighting against the storm, but learning to stand firm in the midst of it.

Zara took a deep breath, inhaling the fresh air, and decided to stay by the water a little longer, allowing herself to reflect on this new understanding of strength. Perhaps, like the lake, she could find a way to let the waves wash over her without letting them drown her.

## What Is Emotional Resilience?

Emotional resilience is the ability to adapt to stressful or traumatic events without allowing them to overwhelm us. It's the capacity to navigate life's challenges—big and small—while maintaining a sense of inner stability and balance. For survivors of trauma, emotional resilience is not about avoiding pain but about learning to weather it, even when it feels like a storm is raging inside.

It's important to note that emotional resilience doesn't mean you won't feel the impacts of trauma; it doesn't mean you'll be impervious to pain or setbacks. Instead, resilience is about building your capacity to face adversity with flexibility—to bend without breaking—and to emerge stronger from life's challenges.

Think of emotional resilience as a muscle. Just as you strengthen your physical muscles through exercise, you can build your emotional resilience through practice. It's about cultivating skills, perspectives, and habits that allow you to bounce back from difficult situations and continue moving forward.

## Cultivating Self-Love: The Foundation of Resilience

At the heart of emotional resilience lies self-love—the practice of valuing, nurturing, and believing in yourself. Trauma often distorts your relationship with yourself, leaving you feeling unworthy or disconnected. Rebuilding this relationship is essential to healing and thriving.

Self-love is not about perfection or selfishness. It's about honoring your needs, respecting your boundaries, and showing yourself the same compassion you'd offer to someone you care about deeply. Here's what self-love looks like in practice:

## 1. Treating Yourself Well

Treating yourself well means prioritizing your physical, emotional, and mental health. It involves recognizing that you deserve care and nourishment, even when life feels overwhelming. Start with small but meaningful acts of kindness toward yourself:

•Nourish Your Body: Feed yourself foods that energize and sustain you. Rest when your body asks for it, and move in ways that feel joyful, not punishing.

•Create a Sanctuary: Make your living space a place that brings you comfort and peace. This could mean lighting a candle, surrounding yourself with meaningful objects, or simply keeping your environment clean and organized.

•Invest in Your Passions: Carve out time for activities that light you up—whether it's painting, gardening, reading, or something else that feeds your soul.

## 2. Talking to Yourself Kindly

The way you speak to yourself matters. Negative self-talk can erode your self-esteem and resilience, while kind, affirming self-talk helps build a solid foundation of self-worth. Pay attention to your inner dialogue. If you notice harsh or critical thoughts, challenge them with compassion.

Try these practices:

•Reframe Your Inner Dialogue: Instead of saying, "I can't believe I messed up again," try, "I made a mistake, but I'm learning and growing."

•Practice Daily Affirmations: Begin each day by saying something kind to yourself, such as, "I am doing my best, and that is enough."

•Forgive Yourself: Remember that you are human, and imperfection is part of the journey. Let go of guilt or shame by reminding yourself that mistakes are opportunities to grow.

## 3. Defending Yourself

Loving yourself also means standing up for your needs, values, and boundaries. It's about protecting your energy and ensuring that you are treated with respect—both by others and by yourself. Defending yourself isn't about aggression; it's about asserting your worth and honoring your boundaries.

Here's how to defend yourself with love:

•Set Boundaries: Clearly communicate what is and isn't acceptable in your relationships. For example, if someone speaks to you disrespectfully, calmly let them know that it's not okay and that you won't tolerate it.

•Say No Without Guilt: Recognize that your time and energy are valuable. Saying "no" to something that drains you is saying "yes" to your well-being.

•Advocate for Your Needs: Whether it's asking for help, speaking up in a meeting, or prioritizing self-care, advocating for your needs reinforces your sense of agency and self-respect.

## 4. Believing in Yourself

Believing in yourself is the ultimate act of self-love. It's about trusting that you have the strength, intelligence, and resilience to navigate life's challenges. Trauma can shake this belief, but rebuilding it is crucial for healing and thriving.

Ways to rebuild belief in yourself:

•Celebrate Your Strengths: Make a list of qualities you admire about yourself. Reflect on your achievements and the challenges you've overcome.

•Visualize Your Future: Imagine the person you want to become and the life you want to create. Visualizing your goals can help you align your actions with your dreams.

•Surround Yourself with Encouragement: Seek out people who uplift and inspire you. Their support can reinforce your belief in yourself when it feels shaky.

## Mindfulness and Emotional Resilience

Mindfulness is another powerful tool in building emotional resilience. It involves paying attention to the present moment without judgment, accepting things as they are without trying to change them. Mindfulness helps you develop greater emotional awareness and control, which is key to building resilience.

When you practice mindfulness, you create a space between stimulus and reaction. Instead of reacting impulsively to emotions or stress, mindfulness allows you to pause, notice your feelings, and choose how to respond. This pause can prevent you from being swept away by your emotions, allowing you to maintain a sense of emotional balance.

## Final Thoughts: Resilience as a Way of Life

Emotional resilience is not something you either have or don't have. It's a practice, a way of engaging with the world that can be developed over time. By practicing self-love, mindfulness, and positive action, you can cultivate resilience that allows you to navigate life's challenges with strength, grace, and clarity.

## Chapter 7: Strengthening Connections

"The best way to find yourself is to lose yourself in the service of others." — Mahatma Gandhi

## The Power of Connection

James sat at the café table, stirring his coffee absentmindedly. The hum of conversation around him was a soothing backdrop, but he felt oddly detached. Socializing, once second nature, had become something he approached with caution. After years of betrayal and mistrust, letting people in again felt risky, like walking a tightrope without a safety net.

Across from him, his friend Mia was sharing updates about her life. Her laughter was warm and familiar, yet James hesitated to fully engage. What if I say the wrong thing? What if I trust her too much? he thought.

But as Mia leaned forward, concern softening her expression, she asked, "How are you really doing?" The genuine care in her voice disarmed James. He realized that connection didn't have to be perfect to be meaningful—it simply needed honesty and effort.

Trust and connection, James reflected, weren't things to be rebuilt overnight. They were gradual, nurtured through small acts of vulnerability and care. As the conversation flowed, he felt a flicker of hope: perhaps, step by step, he could strengthen his relationships and learn to trust again.

## Why Connection Matters

Human beings are wired for connection. It's through our relationships that we find support, understanding, and a sense of belonging. For survivors of trauma, however, connection can feel like a double-edged sword. While relationships have the potential to heal, they also come with the risk of hurt.

Rebuilding trust and strengthening connections after trauma is a brave act. It requires vulnerability, patience, and a willingness to confront fears. But the rewards—deeper intimacy, mutual support, and shared joy—are worth the effort.

## Maslow Before You Bloom

Before you can thrive in higher-level relationships or personal growth, you need to meet your foundational needs. This idea reflects the relationship between Maslow's Hierarchy of Needs and Bloom's Taxonomy of Educational Objectives, which can be summarized as: "You need to Maslow before you Bloom."

Maslow's model outlines a hierarchy of human needs:

1.Physiological needs: Basic survival needs like food, water, and shelter.

2. Safety: A sense of physical and emotional security.

3.Love and belonging: Healthy relationships, social connection, and community.

4.Esteem: Respect, self-worth, and confidence.

5.Self-actualization: Reaching your full potential.

Bloom's Taxonomy, on the other hand, describes higher-order thinking and learning, such as analyzing, evaluating, and creating. However, before you can engage in complex growth or personal transformation (Bloom), you must ensure your basic needs (Maslow) are met.

In relationships, this means:

•You can't expect to thrive in intellectual or emotional intimacy (Bloom) if you don't first feel safe and valued (Maslow).

•Establishing trust, emotional safety, and mutual respect lays the groundwork for deeper connection and shared growth.

For James, rebuilding trust with Mia was about meeting his need for emotional safety first. Once he felt secure in their dynamic, he could open up more fully, allowing their friendship to grow into a source of deeper support and mutual inspiration.

When strengthening connections, ask yourself:

•Do I feel safe in this relationship?

•Do I feel seen, heard, and valued?

•Does this relationship nurture my basic emotional needs?

If the answer is yes, you've established a foundation that allows you to move toward higher levels of connection and shared growth.

**Building Healthy Relationships**

Strong relationships are built on a foundation of trust, respect, and communication. For survivors of trauma, these qualities may feel elusive, but they can be cultivated through intentional actions. Here are some ways to foster healthier, more fulfilling connections:

1. Begin with Self-Trust

Before you can trust others, you must rebuild trust within yourself. This involves recognizing your needs, setting boundaries, and believing that you deserve healthy, respectful relationships. Self-trust forms the foundation for every other connection in your life.

•Listen to Your Instincts: Pay attention to how you feel around certain people. Do they make you feel safe and valued, or do they drain your energy?

•Set Clear Boundaries: Boundaries protect your emotional well-being and ensure your relationships are built on mutual respect. Communicate your limits calmly and assertively.

•Trust Your Ability to Heal: Remind yourself that you have the resilience to navigate relationships, even if they sometimes feel challenging.

## 2. Practice Vulnerability Gradually

Vulnerability is the key to deep connection, but it can feel terrifying after experiencing betrayal or trauma. Start small. Share something personal with someone you trust—a fear, a dream, or a piece of your past. Observe their response. Are they supportive and understanding? Each positive experience of vulnerability reinforces your capacity to connect more deeply.

## 3. Prioritize Mutuality

Healthy relationships are reciprocal. They involve a balance of give and take, where both people feel valued and supported. If a relationship feels one-sided, it may be worth reevaluating its role in your life.

Ask yourself:

•Do I feel safe expressing my feelings with this person?

•Do they listen as much as they talk?

•Do they respect my boundaries and needs?

Mutuality ensures that your relationships are sources of strength rather than stress.

## Navigating Challenges in Relationships

Every relationship, no matter how strong, will face challenges. Conflict is natural and, when handled constructively, can even strengthen bonds. The key is to approach challenges with open communication and a willingness to find solutions together.

Here are some strategies for navigating relationship challenges:

•Stay Present: When conflicts arise, focus on the issue at hand rather than bringing up past grievances.

•Use "I" Statements: Express your feelings without assigning blame. For example, say, "I feel hurt when I'm interrupted," rather than, "You never listen to me."

•Seek Understanding: Approach the conversation with curiosity rather than defensiveness. Ask questions to understand the other person's perspective.

**Final Thoughts: Connection as a Path to Healing**

Strengthening connections after trauma is both challenging and rewarding. It requires vulnerability, self-love, and a willingness to embrace imperfection. But as you rebuild trust and nurture healthy relationships, you'll find that connection becomes one of the most powerful tools in your healing journey.

Remember, you are worthy of relationships that uplift, inspire, and support you. By cultivating self-trust, prioritizing mutuality, and building from a foundation of safety and belonging, you can create connections that not only enrich your life but also help you continue to heal and grow.

## Chapter 8: Reclaiming Your Power

"The most courageous act is still to think for yourself. Aloud." — Coco Chanel

## The Turning Point

Sophia stood in front of the mirror, her hands resting on the edge of the sink. The morning sunlight poured through the window, casting a warm glow over her reflection. But what she saw was not just light—it was strength.

Today was the day she would speak up. After years of silencing her voice and dimming her presence to keep the peace, Sophia had decided she was done living small. The weight of her fears no longer outweighed her desire for freedom. She knew it wouldn't be easy, but reclaiming her power wasn't about perfection—it was about courage.

As she prepared for her meeting, where she would assert her needs and set a long-overdue boundary, Sophia reminded herself of something her therapist had said: "Power isn't about control over others. It's about ownership of your life."

She took a deep breath and whispered to her reflection, "You've got this." For the first time in a long time, she believed it.

## What Does It Mean to Reclaim Your Power?

Reclaiming your power is about taking ownership of your choices, your voice, and your life. Trauma can leave you feeling helpless, as though life is happening to you rather than for you. Reclaiming your power is the process of shifting from passive to active, from reactive to intentional. It's about recognizing your own strength, even when the world tries to convince you otherwise.

Power isn't about dominance or control over others—it's about agency. It's the ability to make decisions that align with your values, advocate for your needs, and stand firm in your worth. This chapter is about rediscovering that agency and taking actionable steps to live a life that reflects your true self.

## The Role of Fear in Disempowerment

Fear is one of the most significant barriers to reclaiming power. After trauma, fear often becomes a constant companion, whispering doubts into your mind and urging you to play small. It convinces you that speaking up will lead to rejection, that setting boundaries will create conflict, and that taking risks will end in failure.

But fear, while powerful, is not insurmountable. It thrives on inaction. The more you avoid facing your fears, the stronger they become. Reclaiming your power involves confronting fear head-on—not by eliminating it, but by acting despite it.

Here's how to begin:

1.Name Your Fear: What is it that you're afraid of? Rejection? Failure? Conflict? Naming your fear helps you see it for what it is—a feeling, not a fact.

2.Challenge the Fear: Ask yourself, What's the worst that could happen? Often, the reality is far less catastrophic than your fear suggests.

3.Take Small Steps: You don't have to leap into the unknown. Start with small, manageable actions that build your confidence over time.

**Self-Advocacy: Owning Your Voice**

Reclaiming your power starts with using your voice. Self-advocacy means speaking up for your needs, values, and boundaries—even when it feels uncomfortable. It's about recognizing that your thoughts and feelings are valid and deserving of expression.

Here are ways to strengthen your self-advocacy:

•Clarify Your Needs: Before you can advocate for yourself, you need to understand what you want. Take time to reflect on your needs, whether they're emotional, physical, or practical.

•Practice Assertive Communication: Use clear, direct language to express your needs. For example, instead of saying, "I guess it's okay if we do it your way," try, "I would prefer to do it this way because it aligns with my goals."

•Stand Firm in Your Boundaries: Advocate for your limits without guilt. Boundaries are not selfish—they're essential for healthy relationships and self-respect.

## Decision-Making as a Form of Power

Trauma often leaves you doubting your ability to make decisions. You may second-guess yourself, fearing that every choice will lead to regret. But reclaiming your power means trusting your intuition and taking responsibility for your path.

To rebuild confidence in your decision-making:

1.Start Small: Begin with low-stakes decisions, like choosing what to eat for dinner or what activity to pursue on a weekend. These small choices help you rebuild trust in your instincts.

2.Weigh Your Values: When making bigger decisions, consider how each option aligns with your core values. Does it move you closer to the life you want to create?

3.Embrace Mistakes: No one makes perfect decisions all the time. Mistakes are not failures—they're opportunities to learn and grow.

## Maslow Before You Bloom: Power and Growth

Reclaiming your power aligns with the concept of Maslow before you Bloom. To thrive and grow (Bloom), you first need to feel secure and supported (Maslow).

Maslow's Hierarchy reminds us that foundational needs like safety, love, and self-esteem must be met before we can achieve self-actualization or personal empowerment. If your life feels unstable—whether due to financial insecurity, unsafe relationships, or unresolved trauma—focusing on those foundational needs is crucial.

Here's how this applies to reclaiming your power:

•Meet Your Basic Needs First: Ensure your physical and emotional safety before taking on new challenges.

•Build Self-Belief: Strengthen your confidence and trust in yourself, which forms the foundation for growth.

•Expand Gradually: Once your foundation feels solid, you can move into higher levels of empowerment—advocating for others, pursuing your passions, and creating lasting change.

This framework reminds us that growth is a process, not a race. Focus on meeting your needs step by step, and you'll find that power naturally follows.

## Letting Go of the Victim Mindset

One of the most empowering shifts you can make is letting go of the victim mindset. This doesn't mean denying the pain or injustice you've experienced—it means refusing to let it define you.

Moving beyond the victim mindset involves:

•Reframing Your Story: See yourself not just as someone who survived trauma, but as someone who is actively rebuilding and thriving.

•Focusing on Agency: Shift your perspective from "Why did this happen to me?" to "What can I do to move forward?"

•Celebrating Small Wins: Every step you take toward reclaiming your power is a victory worth acknowledging.

## Reclaiming Power Through Action

Empowerment is built through action. Each step you take—no matter how small—brings you closer to a life of freedom and authenticity.

Here are ways to take action and reclaim your power:

1.Say No Without Guilt: Recognize that you have the right to prioritize your well-being. Saying "no" to what doesn't serve you is saying "yes" to yourself.

2.Take Up Space: Whether it's sharing your opinion in a meeting or pursuing a passion unapologetically, give yourself permission to be seen and heard.

3.Invest in Yourself: Spend time, energy, and resources on your growth. This could mean taking a class, seeking therapy, or dedicating time to self-care.

### Final Thoughts: Owning Your Life

Reclaiming your power is not a single moment or event—it's a journey of continual growth and self-discovery. It's about choosing, day by day, to live intentionally and authentically, even in the face of fear.

You have the right to take up space, to set boundaries, and to advocate for your needs. You have the strength to make decisions that align with your values. And you have the power to create a life that reflects your worth and potential.

As Sophia reminded herself in the mirror: You've got this.

## Chapter 9: Manifesting Your Vision

"Everything you can imagine is real." — Pablo Picasso

## A Life Worth Creating

Jordan sat at her desk, staring at a blank page in her journal. She had heard so much about the power of visualization and manifesting dreams, but where did she even begin? Her past loomed large, whispering doubts into her mind: You've tried before, and it didn't work. What makes this time different?

But Jordan wasn't the same person she used to be. Months of therapy and self-reflection had taught her that the path forward wasn't about erasing the past—it was about transforming it. She picked up her pen and wrote at the top of the page: My Vision.

Her hand hovered for a moment, and then the words began to flow. "I want a life where I feel peace in the morning. A life where I trust myself to make decisions. A life filled with meaningful connections and creative fulfillment."

As she wrote, a quiet determination rose within her. This wasn't just wishful thinking—it was a declaration. For the first time, she felt not just hope, but agency. Her vision wasn't just a dream; it was a plan waiting to unfold.

**What Does It Mean to Manifest?**

Manifestation is the process of turning your dreams into reality through clarity, intention, and action. It's not magic—it's a partnership between your mindset and your efforts. Trauma can leave you feeling powerless, as though life happens to you rather than for you. Manifesting your vision is about reclaiming that power and actively shaping your future.

At its core, manifestation involves three key elements:

1.Clarity: Knowing what you truly want.

2.Intentionality: Aligning your thoughts, words, and actions with your goals.

3.Action: Taking consistent, purposeful steps toward your vision.

**Singularity Moments: Breakthroughs in Manifestation**

As you work toward manifesting your vision, there will be moments when everything seems to align—when your actions, intentions, and desires come together in a way that feels almost magical. These are singularity moments, the pivotal breakthroughs when your journey shifts dramatically, and your vision begins to take shape.

A singularity moment is the instant when clarity turns into realization, when the effort you've been putting in suddenly feels meaningful, and when your belief in your vision solidifies. These moments are not just milestones—they are transformations, marking a profound shift in how you see yourself and your ability to create the life you desire.

For Jordan, the singularity moment wasn't just writing her vision in the journal. It was the quiet yet powerful realization that her dreams were valid and within reach. That shift—from doubt to belief—was the catalyst for everything that followed.

Singularity moments often arise when:

•You make a bold decision that aligns fully with your values and goals.

•You experience a breakthrough that changes your perspective or eliminates self-doubt.

•The external world begins to reflect the changes you've made internally.

These moments remind you that your vision isn't just possible—it's already unfolding.

**Step 1: Gain Clarity About Your Vision**

Manifesting begins with a clear vision. What kind of life do you want to create? What values do you want to guide your decisions? Clarity isn't just about specific goals; it's about understanding what brings you joy, fulfillment, and peace.

To gain clarity:

•Journal Your Dreams: Write about the life you envision, focusing on how you want to feel. For example, instead of just writing, "I want a better job," explore what a fulfilling career looks and feels like to you.

•Identify Your Core Values: Reflect on what matters most to you—family, creativity, growth, freedom—and let these values guide your vision.

•Release Limiting Beliefs: Notice thoughts that begin with, "I can't," or, "That's not possible for me." Challenge these beliefs with curiosity: "What if I could?"

## Step 2: Align Your Intentions with Your Actions

Intentions are the bridge between your dreams and reality. Setting clear intentions helps you focus your energy and actions toward your goals. But intentions alone aren't enough—they must be followed by purposeful action.

Here's how to align your intentions with your actions:

•Create Daily Rituals: Small, consistent practices keep your vision front and center. This could be a morning affirmation, a nightly journaling session, or a five-minute visualization.

•Prioritize Your Goals: Break your vision into actionable steps. If your goal is to improve your health, for example, start by committing to one small change, like drinking more water or taking a daily walk.

•Practice Gratitude: Gratitude shifts your focus from what's lacking to what's abundant. Reflect on what's already going well in your life to build momentum for the future.

## Step 3: Overcome Barriers with Resilience

The path to manifesting your vision won't be free of obstacles. Fear, self-doubt, and setbacks are natural parts of the journey. Resilience is what keeps you moving forward, even when the road feels uncertain.

Strategies for overcoming barriers:

•Reframe Setbacks: Instead of viewing challenges as failures, see them as opportunities to learn and grow. Ask yourself, "What can this teach me?"

•Build a Support System: Share your vision with trusted friends or mentors who can offer encouragement and accountability.

•Celebrate Progress: Acknowledge every small win, no matter how insignificant it might seem. Progress is cumulative, and every step counts.

## Maslow Before You Bloom: Manifesting with Purpose

The concept of Maslow before you Bloom applies to manifesting as well. You can't effectively create or pursue higher-level goals without a solid foundation of security and well-being.

Here's how this principle plays out:

•Start with Stability: If you're struggling with unmet basic needs—such as financial insecurity or a lack of emotional safety—focus on these areas first. A stable foundation allows you to dream bigger.

•Build Confidence: Strengthen your belief in yourself by celebrating small achievements and reaffirming your ability to grow. Confidence is the bridge between survival and thriving.

•Pursue Growth Mindfully: Once your foundation is solid, explore higher-order goals like personal growth, creativity, or community impact. These pursuits become more fulfilling when they're built on a stable base.

## Manifesting with Self-Love

Manifesting your vision requires not only clarity and action but also self-love. Loving yourself means believing that you are worthy of the life you dream of and treating yourself with care and compassion throughout the journey.

Here's how self-love supports manifestation:

•Treat Yourself Kindly: When you encounter setbacks, avoid self-criticism. Instead, remind yourself that growth takes time.

•Defend Your Dreams: Advocate for your vision, even if others doubt or question it. Your dreams are valid and deserve respect.

•Celebrate Your Efforts: Acknowledge the courage it takes to dream big and the dedication it takes to pursue those dreams.

### Final Thoughts: A Vision Worth Living

Manifesting your vision is not just about achieving goals—it's about creating a life that aligns with your values, passions, and purpose. Singularity moments will mark your journey, reminding you of your strength and the beauty of alignment.

As Jordan discovered, your vision is more than a dream—it's a declaration of your worth and potential. With clarity, self-love, resilience, and trust in those singularity moments, you can transform your vision into a reality that reflects the life you deserve.

# Chapter 10: Living Your Empowered Life

"You are allowed to be both a masterpiece and a work in progress simultaneously." — Sophia Bush

## From Ashes to Empowerment

Riley stood at the threshold of her apartment, suitcase in hand. It wasn't just a trip—it was a declaration. She had spent the last two years rebuilding her life, and now, for the first time in as long as she could remember, she felt ready to explore the world again. Trauma had taught her to fear change, but healing had taught her to embrace it.

As the taxi pulled up, she felt a flicker of doubt, a small whisper from her past: Are you sure you can do this? But Riley had learned how to respond to that voice. She placed her hand over her heart, took a deep breath, and whispered back, "I've got this. I'm stronger than I think."

This wasn't just a moment of courage—it was a singularity moment. Riley was stepping into her empowered life, where her past no longer dictated her future, and her dreams were no longer deferred.

## What Does an Empowered Life Look Like?

Living an empowered life doesn't mean you'll never face challenges or doubts again. It means you've built the tools, confidence, and resilience to navigate them with grace and determination. Empowerment is about reclaiming your narrative, making choices that align with your values, and showing up for yourself every day.

An empowered life is one where:

•You treat yourself with kindness and respect.

•You trust your decisions and stand by your boundaries.

•You pursue growth with courage and curiosity.

•You find purpose in your experiences, even the painful ones.

## The Journey of Becoming

The path to living an empowered life isn't linear—it's an ongoing process of growth and self-discovery. Every step you've taken in this book has laid the groundwork for this transformation. From rebuilding trust to manifesting your vision, you've learned to turn adversity into strength and doubt into belief.

Here's how to sustain and deepen your empowerment:

## 1. Embrace Continual Growth

Empowerment isn't a destination; it's a journey of continual learning and evolution. As you grow, your needs, goals, and vision may shift. Embracing this fluidity allows you to stay aligned with your true self.

•Adopt a Growth Mindset: See challenges as opportunities to learn rather than obstacles to avoid. Remind yourself, "I can grow from this."

•Reflect Regularly: Set aside time to reflect on your journey—what's working, what needs adjustment, and what new goals excite you.

•Celebrate Milestones: Acknowledge the progress you've made, whether it's a small win or a major breakthrough. Every step matters.

## 2. Cultivate Gratitude and Presence

Gratitude is a powerful tool for staying grounded in the present while appreciating how far you've come. By focusing on what's good in your life, you reinforce a sense of abundance and possibility.

•Practice Daily Gratitude: Each day, write down three things you're grateful for, no matter how small. This practice shifts your focus from what's missing to what's meaningful.

•Stay Present: Avoid getting lost in the "what-ifs" of the future or the "if-onlys" of the past. Mindfulness keeps you connected to the here and now, where your power lies.

## 3. Turn Pain into Purpose

Your past doesn't define you, but it can shape your purpose. Many people who have overcome trauma find meaning in helping others, creating art, or advocating for change. Turning pain into purpose is a profound act of empowerment.

Ask yourself:

•What has my journey taught me?

•How can I use my experiences to inspire or support others?

•What brings me fulfillment and joy?

Whether it's sharing your story, mentoring someone, or pursuing a passion project, channeling your experiences into something meaningful reinforces your sense of agency and worth.

## 4. Build a Legacy of Empowerment

An empowered life isn't just about personal growth—it's about creating a ripple effect. When you live authentically and courageously, you inspire others to do the same.

Here's how to build your legacy:

•Model Empowerment: Show others what's possible by living in alignment with your values and dreams.

•Share Your Wisdom: Mentor or support those who are just beginning their healing journey. Your insight could be the catalyst for someone else's transformation.

•Contribute to Your Community: Whether through volunteering, advocacy, or creative expression, find ways to give back and make a positive impact.

## Singularity Moments: The Turning Points of Empowerment

An empowered life is marked by singularity moments—those pivotal breakthroughs when your growth and alignment become undeniable. These moments are often unexpected but transformative, signaling that you've stepped into your power.

A singularity moment might be:

•The day you set a boundary and felt no guilt.

•The first time you pursued a dream despite fear.

•A quiet realization that your worth isn't tied to your past.

These moments are reminders of your strength and resilience. They serve as milestones on your journey, showing how far you've come and inspiring you to keep moving forward.

5. Live with Intention

Intentionality is the cornerstone of an empowered life. It means making conscious choices that reflect your values and priorities, rather than living on autopilot.

•Align Your Actions with Your Values: Before making a decision, ask yourself, "Does this align with the life I want to create?"

•Practice Self-Compassion: Living with intention doesn't mean perfection. When you make a misstep, treat yourself with kindness and learn from the experience.

•Create Rituals of Empowerment: Develop daily or weekly practices that keep you connected to your goals and vision, such as journaling, meditation, or affirmations.

## Maslow Before You Bloom: Empowerment in Layers

As you live your empowered life, remember the concept of Maslow before you Bloom. Even in empowerment, foundational needs must be nurtured before you can fully thrive.

•Tend to Your Foundations: Regularly check in with your basic needs—physical, emotional, and relational—and ensure they're being met.

•Expand Mindfully: With a solid foundation, you can explore higher levels of growth, creativity, and contribution.

•Honor the Process: Growth happens in layers. Be patient with yourself as you move through different stages of empowerment.

### The Power of Believing in Yourself

Perhaps the greatest act of empowerment is believing in your own worth and potential. This belief is what fuels resilience, courage, and action. It's what allows you to face challenges with confidence and pursue your dreams with determination.

Here's how to cultivate self-belief:

•Celebrate Your Strengths: Reflect on the qualities that have brought you this far—your resilience, kindness, creativity, or perseverance.

•Reframe Doubts: When self-doubt arises, challenge it with evidence of your growth. Remind yourself, "I've overcome so much—I can handle this too."

•Visualize Your Future Self: Imagine the empowered person you're becoming and the life you're creating. Let this vision guide your actions and decisions.

## Your Empowered Life Starts Now

Living an empowered life isn't about having all the answers or never facing challenges. It's about showing up for yourself, day after day, with courage and intention. It's about believing that you are worthy of love, joy, and fulfillment—and taking action to make that belief a reality.

As Riley stepped into the taxi, she wasn't leaving her past behind—she was carrying its lessons with her, transforming them into fuel for her future. Like Riley, you are ready to step into your empowered life, where every decision reflects your worth, every action honors your growth, and every moment is an opportunity to live authentically.

Your journey has brought you here. The next chapter is yours to write.

"Healing is not an overnight process. It is a journey, a journey that requires patience and acceptance." — Anonymous

Further Reading and References

1.    Bloom, B. S., Engelhart, M. D., Furst, E. J., Hill, W. H., & Krathwohl, D. R. (1956). Taxonomy of Educational Objectives: The Classification of Educational Goals. Handbook I: Cognitive Domain. New York: David McKay.

2.    Brown, B. (2010). The Gifts of Imperfection: Let Go of Who You Think You're Supposed to Be and Embrace Who You Are. Hazelden Publishing.

3.    Caine, C. (2016). Unstoppable: Step Into Your Purpose, Run Your Race, Embrace the Future. Zondervan.

4.    Doidge, N. (2007). The Brain That Changes Itself: Stories of Personal Triumph from the Frontiers of Brain Science. Penguin Books.

5.    Frankl, V. E. (1946). Man's Search for Meaning. Beacon Press.

6.    Kabat-Zinn, J. (1994). Wherever You Go, There You Are: Mindfulness Meditation in Everyday Life. Hachette Books.

7.      Levine, P. A. (1997). Waking the Tiger: Healing Trauma. North Atlantic Books.

8.      Maslow, A. H. (1943). A Theory of Human Motivation. Psychological Review, 50(4), 370–396.

9.      National Institute of Mental Health (NIMH). (2020). Post-Traumatic Stress Disorder Fact Sheet. Retrieved from NIMH.gov.

10.     Rumi. The Essential Rumi. (Translations by Coleman Barks). HarperOne.

11.     van der Kolk, B. A. (2014). The Body Keeps the Score: Brain, Mind, and Body in the Healing of Trauma. Viking.

12.     Williamson, M. (1992). A Return to Love: Reflections on the Principles of A Course in Miracles. HarperOne.

Made in the USA
Columbia, SC
15 January 2025

50843753R00046